Lost in Space

By Kerri Lane
Illustrated by Marc Lynch

Pearson Australia
(a division of Pearson Australia Group Pty Ltd)
707 Collins Street, Melbourne, Victoria 3008
PO Box 23360, Melbourne, Victoria 8012
www.pearson.com.au

First published 2014 by Pearson Australia
2020 2019 2018 2017
10 9 8 7 6 5 4 3 2 1

Publisher: Kieren Noonan
Project Managers: Tamara Pirois and Rachel Davis
Lead Editors: Kerry Nagle and Beth Zeme
Editor: Carolyn Glascodine
Cover and Series Designers: Jenny Grigg and Anne Donald
Designers: Nina Heryanto and Leigh Ashforth
Copyright & Pictures Editor: Julia Weaver
Mac Operator: Rob Curulli
Cover art: Marc Lynch
Illustrator: Marc Lynch
Printed in Australia by the SOS Print + Media Group

ISBN 978 1 4860 0755 4

Pearson Australia Group Pty Ltd ABN 40 004 245 943

Acknowledgements
Every effort has been made to trace and acknowledge copyright. However, if any infringement has occurred, the publishers tender their apologies and invite the copyright holders to contact them.

Disclaimer

Some of the images used in *Lost in Space* might have associations with deceased Indigenous Australians. Please be aware that these images might cause sadness or distress in Aboriginal or Torres Strait Islander communities.

Contents

Chapter 1

Blast off!

Sometimes dreams can seem so real that you really think they're happening. This one was a beauty, and I never wanted it to end. It was about a spaceship – and it was the coolest dream I'd ever had. I love space! Not to mention spaceships and planets and every single thing about the great beyond. Yes, this was, without a doubt, my kind of dream!

The ship shimmered in the moonlight, all silver and lime green, my favourite colours. But then again, dreams probably give you what you want to see, right? Well, good dreams do.

And this was definitely a good one. The best dream ever! Right up until I stepped on the bindi.

"Ouch!"

A bindi? Since when do dreams have bindis? I grabbed my foot and pulled out the little brown spike, which felt *very* real.

Blinking, I looked around. I was in my backyard, it was night time and I was in my PJs. In my dream, I'd been about to reach out and touch the spaceship … then I reached out and *actually* touched the spaceship. I expected it to be cool, but it was warm, like the bonnet of a car just after it has parked.

I looked around for someone, anyone, to make sure I wasn't seeing things. But the only one around was Rover, our dog, and he was snoring loudly enough to wake the neighbours. I pinched myself to check I definitely wasn't dreaming.

"Double ouch!"

That really hurt. This was no dream!

How cool! There I was, standing in my PJs in my own backyard, in front of a spaceship. The spaceship seemed empty and had a miniscule door hanging open, ready for someone to crawl right into. Someone like me!

The spaceship wasn't one of those pancake-shaped things. This one was shaped like a rocket. For a microsecond I thought about waking up Mum and Dad to show them. They were astronomers, so I knew they'd be shocked to see a spaceship in our backyard. After all, they were the ones who taught me everything I know about space.

You could say I am a little obsessed with space. I have practically grown up with a telescope attached to my eye, looking out into space, dreaming about travelling there when I became old enough to be an astronaut. I know more about space than anyone else in my entire school. OK, so there are only fifty kids at my school, but I still know more than any of them, teachers included!

This wasn't the time to race back into the house and wake Mum and Dad, though. There wasn't a moment to waste. I, Caelan James Rex Mantash, had to find out more about this mystery spaceship. I lurched forward, trying to avoid any more bindis, and headed for the spaceship's door.

The inside was honestly enough to take your breath away. Around me were trillions of lights, set into dashboards. They lined the counters that ran around under the huge windscreen, a big, long window that a space traveller could use to view whatever world they explored next.

There was a drop-down wall with a map of the solar system. On the floor around the ship, there were telescopes, machines with flashing lights, a strange tube that looked like a type of thermometer, with bright yellow goo inside, and cupboards bulging with things that beeped or moved. I wanted to inspect everything, but I didn't know where to start.

Desperate to take it all in, I stepped backwards and got the fright of my life! Two electronic arms came out and shoved a tray at me. On the tray sat a jug of milky blue liquid and a triangular cup.

A robot! And it was as big as me! I hadn't even seen it lurking in the shadows.

"*Matoo, kikokaffan*?" enquired the robot. Was it offering me a drink? Wispy blue steam trailed from the jug. It looked like alien tea!

I'm no coward, but I'm not about to take unnecessary risks either. I started to back away, but the robot trundled after me. To my astonishment, the robot started pouring the liquid all over the floor in front of me, not into the cup.

Maybe it was time to get out. But just as I started for the hatch I'd crawled through, I heard some high-pitched voices, which sounded like they were arguing with each other. Then I heard a noise that sounded like engines starting up.

And then I felt it. The thrust. The spaceship was moving! I tried to grab hold of something, but I was too slow.

Next thing I knew I'd been shoved back onto my butt by the force. My head hit the side of the bench – hard. We were really travelling!

A shot of panic raced through me. Then a teeny trickle of something slipped down my face. I wiped it away, but not before the colour caught my eye.

Blood?

I didn't feel faint, so it must have just been a small bump on the head. But the sight of blood reminded me that this was *definitely* no dream. I'd been kidnapped by aliens, who probably tricked me into climbing on board so they could examine my superior brain! What was I going to do now? How would I get back home? And what would my parents do once they discovered I was missing? They'd go crazy!

HELP!

Chapter 2

Monsters ahoy!

I searched for somewhere to hide in the spaceship, but there weren't many options. The cupboards were full and I couldn't exactly hide behind the robot, who was still trying to pour tea for me. I dived under a control panel just as two 'things' ran in, still arguing! One of them absently flicked a switch on the robot as it passed and all the robot's lights went out as it shut down. But that wasn't what was worrying me! What worried me was that I'd never seen beings like them before. They really were aliens!

I couldn't help it! I screeched. It was a long, loud, spine-tingling screech, and as soon as it hit the air, I knew I'd made a mistake. Both the 'things' stopped and spun around, their eyes – *one on each of them* – growing wider than the Moon as they spotted me huddled under one of the control panels.

They approached me cautiously, looked down at me, apparently examining me very closely. My heart thumped so loudly in my chest that it felt like my ears were going to pop. I wanted to scream, but my mouth was dry, and I couldn't make a sound, so screamed silently.

I looked frantically for an escape route, but through the big, long windscreen, I could see that the Universe was flying past at warp speed!

The aliens started screaming. "*Mompotz! Mompotz!*" they cried. I couldn't tell if they were excited or scared.

This was crazy! Why were they doing that? What started out as a cool dream had turned into a very nasty real-life kidnapping.

I was trapped in a strange spaceship with two one-eyed, one-toothed, mini monsters!

Finally, they stopped screaming at me. They were clinging to each other, backing up slowly until they hit the cupboard behind them. Their screams had lowered to little whimpers, but their many arms were still shaking like jelly snakes that had come alive. One of them had five arms and was slightly taller, with purple skin. The other was smaller in height, had four arms and green skin. And they were talking in some strange language, which sounded just like the one the tea robot had used. An *alien* language. What hope did I have of getting home *now*, if I couldn't even talk to these two?

One of them spoke. "*Chizool Zeet!*" The other one appeared to nod.

At my startled look, the other one thumped its mate, and they both fiddled with dials that sat just above some small computer screens strapped to their chests. The first alien spoke again.

"We caught one!" It said to its partner. Then it turned to me. "What is your name?"

My eyes popped. The dial on its chest was a translator!

"My … name? It's Caelan Mantash. Who are you?"

"I'm Klingzong," said the purple one, "and I'm the tallest girl in my class."

The green one rolled its eye.

"I'm Elvis," it said, "And tall girls annoy me. A lot." Klingzong glared at him.

"Only a boy would say that," she said. "A short one."

"Your name is Elvis?" I gasped.

Elvis rolled his eye again. "We found you on planet Earth, didn't we? My mother was accidentally teleported to your planet for a while, many years ago. She never forgot Elvis …" His lip curled as he finished his speech, and my eyes completely bugged out when he did a little hip twist, just like I'd seen Elvis Presley do.

"Why have you kidnapped me?" I asked.

"We'd never kidnap a monster like you!" Klingzong scoffed. "We've simply *borrowed* you for our school science presentation, to prove to everyone that we know a lot about space!"

"I think I know more about space than either of you two!" I said. "My parents are astronomers. And just who are you calling a monster? I'm not the one with five arms and one eye stuck in the middle of his head!"

At this point I was still crouched on the floor of the spaceship, so I pulled myself up, which prompted another screech from the aliens."You're hideous! We were warned about monsters like you," Klingzong sobbed.

I was about to argue when something caught my eye. Suddenly, arguing about who was the ugliest didn't seem important, because what I was seeing outside the window was far worse.

"Um … Who's driving this thing? And how fast are we going?" I asked nervously, pointing out the window.

"Why should we tell *you*?" Elvis snapped.

I dived around the room, looking for some kind of control.

"Because if you don't, we're going to end up as fried as an egg!" I cried. "See that orangey-red thing?" I pointed frantically out the window. "That's Venus! That means we're probably on a collision course with the SUN!"

They both peered at the map of the solar system on the wall. "Which one's the Sun?" Elvis asked.

I gasped, horrified. I'd already forgotten that I was probably the only one on this spaceship with astronomers for parents. "The Sun is the life source for planet Earth and the largest body in the solar system. But it's also the thing that's going to turn us into barbecued spare ribs! Do you get it? It's a massive fiery ball of gas that's burning at sixteen million degrees Celsius at its core and over five and a half thousand degrees on the surface!"

Klingzong did a quick calculation on her chest pad and then her eye flew open. "Arghhhhh!" she squealed.

Elvis had the exact same reaction. "That's h . . . h . . . hot!" he cried. "So, what about this Venus place? Just head for that?" He rushed forward and began to push almost every button he could see on the control panel, his one eye swivelling rapidly.

"Yeah, right!" I said. "Great plan! That way we'll only take a half second to fry instead of a tenth of a second!"

"Huh?" Klingzong said.

"Do you guys know *anything* about the Milky Way?" I asked, shocked.

"Yes, of course!" Elvis began, but Klingzong poked him with one of her elbows, and they both shook their heads. I would have sighed if I hadn't been so afraid.

"Venus is the second hottest planet! Its surface temperature is more than 460 degrees Celsius! Either way, we're cooked!"

Klingzong rolled her eye around the room. "I'm too young to be cooked! I'm only 1305 years old! Quick! What do we do?"

"You're asking me?" I yelled back. "This is your spaceship!"

"No, it isn't," Elvis yelled back. "It's our neighbour's. We borrowed it so we could find a space monster and finish our science presentation. We don't really know how to drive it. We don't even have our spaceship licences! And now we've flown so far away from home that we can't even call our mother and get her to find us and take us home again!" The lower lips of both of the aliens began to quiver pathetically.

"You *what*?" I bellowed. This couldn't be happening!

"It's not our fault the navigation computer isn't working!" said Klingzong. "Or that we don't know how to regulate the speed! We nearly crashed! We were just lucky that this ship has the latest parking technology when we happened to land on your planet and catch you."

How was I going to stop us from flying into the Sun? I had to try and save us and get myself back home before my parents found out I had been kidnapped. Otherwise, we were going to be toasted – by the Sun!

I realised we had nothing to lose, so I began pushing or pulling on any control that looked like it might be a navigation device.

"Quickly!" Elvis screamed. "Venus is getting closer!" I glanced up to see the aliens' bright purple and green faces turning unattractive shades of lilac. My own face must have been ghostly white.

"How fast are we going?" I yelled. "Forget it!" I continued. "I found the speedo!" It read 50 000 000 kilometres per hour! How could anything go that fast?!

My heart was still thumping and my hands were shaking, but I had to force my mind to think.

When I did begin to think, the calculations I made were very worrying. Venus was 108 million kilometres away from the Sun. Earth was over 149 million kilometres away from the Sun. And I figured we'd already been travelling for twenty minutes.

Oh no! That meant we'd be slicing right through the Sun in *less than forty minutes*!

It was already starting to get *much* hotter in the cabin. With their jelly-like bodies, my alien travellers were starting to look like slowly melting butter.

"Quick! Start pulling levers and pushing buttons!" I cried. At least the aliens' extra arms could come in handy for something.

But that still didn't mean we'd find the navigator in time …

Chapter 3

Too close for comfort!

I was dripping sweat over all the lights and buttons on the dashboard. I shot from one end of the control panel to the other as I tried to stop us from melting. Suddenly, as I pulled one lever towards me, I heard a change in the engine. Yes! We were slowing down! I dragged the lever harder to slow us more. Frantically, I hit more buttons and levers and felt the spaceship shift. We were changing direction!

When we finally veered away from the Sun, I flopped back in the chair that was bolted to the floor and closed my eyes with relief.

When I opened my eyes again, I saw the two aliens curled up together with their hands over their eyes, like kittens getting ready to go to sleep.

"Is it safe to look yet?" Klingzong asked, pulling a slightly shaky hand from his eye.

I shook my head. "I don't get you guys! I'm the one who should be scared! This is your territory even if it isn't your spaceship!"

Elvis stood up and hung his head. "No, it's not. We know plenty of things about *our* galaxy, but only a little about this one. When we took the ship to find a space monster, we were going to bring the spaceship back before anyone knew we'd taken it. But we kind of got lost."

"We're going to be in so much trouble," Klingzong said. "Mum said if I did one more thing wrong, she wasn't going to let me play spaceball for a whole month. I'll miss the finals!"

I stared at Klingzong. "I thought you said you were 1305 years old?"

"We are!" they both chorused. Klingzong unclipped the screen on her chest and began to tap on it quickly. "It says that it takes three whole Earth days for our planet to revolve around our sun."

I laughed. "That means that each one of *your* years is only three of Earth's days. Our planet takes 365 days to orbit our life source!" I said. Then I paused, shocked. "Wait ... does that mean you're 10.7 years old in human years? Hey! I'm older than you! I'm eleven!'

"Pleased to meet you, Eleven," said Klingzong.

"But my name's not eleven. It's Caelan, remember?"

"That's right! Kaylan, Kaylan ..." Klingzong continued tapping her screen. It made a horrible beeping sound every time she couldn't find information about my name. She gave up, shrugged, and pointed to Elvis.

"Are you like him or like me?"

"What do you mean?" I asked.

"Are you a boy, like Elvis, or a girl, like me?"

"I'm like Elvis. I'm a boy."

"Pfft!" Elvis scoffed. "I'm not like you at all!" He turned sideways so I could appreciate his profile. "Can't you tell? I'm a very *handsome* boy! I won the beautiful baby contest back in 26 300 005."

Klingzong rolled her eyes again and put one set of hands on her hips.

"You did not!" She said.

"I did too!"

"You only got runner-up!"

I watched in horror as they started pushing each other, with each shove becoming harder and harder …

"Hey, you two! Come on, this could be dangerous!" The last thing I needed was more delay. I needed to get home as soon as I could. If my parents discovered me missing, it would be a disaster of planetary proportions!

Too late! A final shove sent Klingzong sailing across the cabin.

One of her arms caught a big purple lever set apart from the others. Before I could even utter a word, the whole ship started shuddering.

Images raced through my mind. I'd seen this happen on the space program shows. It was an emergency procedure in case of fire. The ship was getting ready to expel its engines! We'd never get home!

My dive beat all speed records as I launched myself on the lever, pushing it back and hoping I wasn't too late. Barely able to breathe, I waited, hearing the system go into reverse. Then I heard the *clonk* of locks sliding back into place.

Relief washed through me like a tidal wave. *Phew!* Worn out, I slumped back into my chair. That was close! If I hadn't been able to stop that, we'd have been free-floating forever! Or until we ran out of supplies … and died from lack of food and water!

That brought me to another question:

What did aliens eat, and would I be able to eat it too?

Elvis frowned at me from across the room. "You look a bit green, Caelan. Want me to let in some fresh space air?"

What?

Chapter 4

Not too hot, not too cold – just right

He couldn't mean … ? He did! Elvis had waddled over to the door and was pulling the release!

The instant suction was like a reverse cyclone! We were going to get sucked into the holding area, and then pushed out into space like space garbage!

"Nooooo!" I screamed. "Hang on! Grab anything!" I clung to the chair, feeling the force drag at me. It pulled at my body, my face, my clothes. My heart raced; any minute now I was going to be floating in space.

Floating in space without oxygen, without a space suit! That meant …

"Help! I'm slipping!" I shouted.

"Ooohhh, me too!" Klingzong cried.

The roaring noise of the vacuum blasted my eardrums, but the voices of the aliens still reached me. Straining, I tried to turn towards them, but the force of the suction held me firm. Then I saw it! A green scaly arm sliding past me! Then a head! Klingzong had two arms wrapped around my chair and another stretched out, hanging onto Elvis, who was right on the edge of the cabin!

Space, as black as ink, swirled around outside the holding area door, which was seconds away from opening and sucking all three of us out into space.

With as much strength as I could muster, I reached down to link my arm around Klingzong's and yelled into what I thought was her ear. "Link one arm around my leg too! I'll try to pull you both back!"

Feeling her grab me and hang on for her life, I heaved backwards. Every muscle screamed, but the pull of the suction was too strong! The chair started to strain against the bolts … We were going … I couldn't stop it!

Then … *oomph*! Something hit the ship, rocking it violently and knocking the wind from my lungs.

"Now we're being attacked!" screamed Elvis.

I struggled to hold on, but it was too late. The ship tipped and I was flung backwards, straight towards the holding area! The aliens screamed as we all sailed through the air. My hands were flailing, desperately searching for anything to hold on to.

As my hands hit the control panel, I felt something and held tight, but I wasn't strong enough and it slipped from my hand. Oh no! I continued to tumble, with no idea about what was happening!

Suddenly, I heard whoops of laughter. "You did it, Caelan!"

As I thumped onto the floor, I realised the suction had stopped. My eyes went first to the doors, which were now safely closed, and then to the control panel. I'd grabbed the emergency door lever, completely by accident!

So, what had hit us? Looking out through the huge 360-degree windscreen of the spaceship, I saw a gigantic rock right alongside us. Still shaking, I reached out to the steering control and gently pulled the spaceship to the left, moving us away.

"We're not being attacked. That's an asteroid. They're left over from when the solar system was created. They just float around in space." I dragged in a deep, calming breath. "In fact, this one saved us …"

The aliens didn't look convinced. Elvis shuddered. "Your solar system is a very dangerous place! I'd hate to be lost out here alone!"

Klingzong pulled herself to her feet and bopped Elvis on the head with one of her arms. "We *are* lost out here alone!"

"No, we're not!" argued Elvis. "Caelan plays here all the time, don't you, Caelan?"

My eyes were so wide they were going to pop. "Me? *Play here?* This is space! Outer space! The furthest I've ever been is to Sydney and we went there by train!"

"Is that a 'no', then?" Elvis asked sweetly. When I nodded, his face immediately changed from sweet to terrified and he ran around the cabin, screaming.

"We'll never get home! We're doomed! We're lost forever! We'll starve! We'll ..." The screaming stopped. "Oh wait," he called. "No need to panic! I just found some Rocko Pops! Anyone for breakfast?"

Klingzong stormed after him, snatching away the box of cereal.

"We have to pace ourselves," she said. "We must ration the food!"

Elvis's big green lip dropped. "You're so mean. And I'm *not* going to share my last jelly baby! So there!" He pulled out something purple and squishy that looked a bit like a jelly baby – *except it looked exactly like Klingzong and Elvis* – popped it into his mouth and chewed noisily. "Hmm, delicious!"

I sniffed the air. The jelly baby smelled like rotten egg. They liked that flavour? I definitely couldn't eat their food, then! But that was the least of my worries. Klingzong and Elvis were right. We still had to find our way home. And I had to get back before my parents started searching the stars for me.

For a few minutes I just stared out into the darkness. The stars were so bright! They were like trillions of diamonds, floating on black velvet. It was beautiful, but now I just wanted to go back home. Could I?

All my thoughts were pushed aside when Klingzong spoke again, after several minutes of whispering between the two aliens.

"We've had an idea!" she boasted. "And I don't know why *you* didn't think of it!"

"What idea?" I asked, worried.

"This one!" Elvis said, as he pointed to the map of the solar system on the wall.

"There are eight planets in your solar system. Is that correct?" Klingzong said.

I nodded.

"Well," she continued in a sing-song voice, "if Earth is so primitive that it doesn't have Space Taxis, then why don't we just drop in on one of the other seven planets and get directions? Maybe someone could fly us home!"

I laughed so hard I could hardly stand up. The two aliens just stared. Their single, googly eyes rolled from one another, back to me and then started over again.

"Did we say something funny?" Elvis asked in a cool tone.

"Yes! Very funny!" I finally got out. "You can't just land on any of those other planets! As far as we know, there are no life forms other than on Earth!"

They gasped.

"The planets near Earth don't have life.

Some planets in our solar system are made up of snow, gas and dust. Planets that *aren't* like this are called rocky planets. Earth's a rocky planet. Venus, Mercury and Mars are too. They're made up of dust, iron and snow."

"So, why aren't we going to those planets?" Elvis asked, as if he was talking to a child.

"Well, for starters, Venus and Mercury are way too hot!" I replied in the same tone.

Klingzong marched closer to the map and shoved the ninth finger of her third hand right up against Mars. "We'll head to Mars then."

I shook my head in frustration. "It's not that easy! Mars is too cold!"

Elvis rolled his eye, wandered over to a cupboard that turned out to be a mini fridge, and pulled out a bottle of thick brown stuff that looked like mud. "*Some planets are too hot and some are too cold!*" he said. "This is sounding more and more like *Boldilocks* every second!"

I shrugged. "And Earth is just right. It's why it has life on it."

"How do you remember all this stuff?" Klingzong asked.

"Easy!" I told them. "Just make up a saying."

"What kind of saying?" Elvis asked.

"I have one that uses the first letters of all the planets." I said. "I put the Sun first so I know which planet is closest to it: **S**o, **M**y **V**ery **E**xcellent **M**other **J**ust **S**ent **U**s **N**achos."

I nodded at the map. "See? Sun: Mercury, Venus, Earth, Mars, Jupiter, Saturn, Uranus and Neptune. Mercury is the closest to the Sun, so it revolves fastest, and Neptune is the furthest away, so it takes the longest to revolve around the Sun!"

"All very interesting," Klingzong said in a desperate voice, "but I can't see how it helps us to find our way home."

I felt my shoulders slump. She was right. It had been fun talking about the planets and sharing what I knew, but it wasn't helping us one little bit.

Outside the windscreen, a scorchingly hot comet whizzed past. All my life I'd wished I could see one up close and there it was. This one was a dirty snowball with a long, fiery tail. At that moment, I wished I could just grab hold of that tail and let it take me home.

Except, I realised with a jolt, that it was probably headed towards the Sun.

I looked across at my fellow travellers who were now wrestling over another Jelly Alien that Elvis had pulled from his pocket. They were weird, but they probably weren't that bad.

I thought again about getting home before my parents found out I'd been kidnapped. This was my chance to make that happen. Without thinking, I lunged for what I thought was the right lever …

Chapter 5

Home, sweet ... aahhhh!

I wasn't sure what I'd done. One minute everything was going along smoothly, and the next we were all upside down! Floating! Somehow we were suddenly in an anti-gravity zone!

There must be something that blocks the anti-gravity and allows us to function normally. Instead, we were weightless! At any other time this might have been fun, but I was over it! I'd had enough!

Especially when I glanced out the windscreen. There, right in front of us, was another planet.

I should have realised this would happen – after all, *we* were moving and the *planets* were moving!

I recognised this planet instantly. I'd know those coloured rings anywhere! Saturn! All the planets had them, but Saturn's were spectacular. My brain scanned what I knew about Saturn. I knew it wasn't going to barbecue us, but ...

Freeze us!

Yes! I remembered. Saturn has a surface temperature of about minus 180 degrees Celsius! That's about 180 degrees below freezing! Unless I could get to those controls, we were about to be turned into snowmen!

"Quick!" I shouted. "Help me! We have to change direction again!"

The other two looked out the window the minute I spoke. As expected, they started squealing.

"Just help me!" I shouted, dog paddling in mid-air, trying to get myself upright again.

You can get somewhere dog paddling in water, but with no gravity, I wasn't getting anywhere.

"What are you doing?" Klingzong called.

"Dog paddling!" I said. Before I could say anything else, they'd pulled out their screens and were looking up 'dog'. Did they have to do that *now*?

Obviously they did – and they also had to bark! So there we were, all three of us floating in mid-air, while two of us barked like seasick pooches and we hurtled towards Saturn!

This was getting us nowhere! At my urging, Klingzong and Elvis grabbed an arm each and tried to push me forward, but I barely moved. Then Elvis did a somersault and I had an idea.

"Stay there!" I called. "I'm coming down!" Elvis's head was near my feet, so I grabbed his hands and somersaulted over him. "Climb down over me. Klingzong, you grab my head and keep pushing down. When I climb down over Elvis, you climb down over me! We'll create a living rope. OK?"

And amazingly, it worked!

When Klingzong reached the controls, she anchored herself to the bolted-down chair and hung on with two arms, pulling me down with her other three arms. Finally, we were there! We'd made it back to the controls! The aliens wrapped their many arms around anything solid, while holding me as well. Now I just had to find that navigation lever again!

When I found it, and we again started to shift away from danger, I didn't even have time to feel relief, because I had to start looking for the solution to the next problem – getting gravity back in this cabin – immediately!

"Are there any more surprises I need to watch out for?"

"Just the button that releases the wild *gorilla-sauruses*," Klingzong said.

"*What!*" More sweat started forming on my forehead.

They both grinned from where they'd floated back up to the ceiling.

"Just kidding," Klingzong said. "By the way, I'd try that green lever. I'm pretty sure that's the one."

I held my breath. What if it was wrong? But what if it was the right one? Closing my eyes, I pulled. I opened them when I heard the two loud thumps and a lot of "ouches".

It had worked. Klingzong and Elvis were now off the ceiling. And I couldn't help but smile. What happened next made me smile even more.

Klingzong waddled over to look at the lever. Next to the lever was a tiny button, and when she saw it, she gasped.

"I think that's the button for the navigation system, and it's turned off!" She said. "We must have bumped it."

The answer to our problems had been under our noses the entire time!

I turned on the navigation system and set it to 27 Blackburn Street, Boot Bay, Queensland, Australia, Earth, the Milky Way galaxy.

27 BLACKBURN ST,
BOOT BAY
QUEENSLAND,
AUSTRALIA,
EARTH,
THE MILKY WAY
GALAXY

Soon, I'd be home. I couldn't believe just how happy that thought made me. I could only hope my parents hadn't spotted that I wasn't sleeping in my bed. After I got back to my house, I'd set the navigation system so my two alien travellers could get back home.

"By the way," I asked, the happiest I'd been since I wandered into this spaceship, "Where do you live?"

I was staring at two blank faces. I felt a deep, sick feeling in my stomach. "Please don't tell me you don't know where you live!" I cried incredulously.

Klingzong shrugged. "Okay, we won't tell you."

Elvis stretched up and threw his arm over my shoulder.

"So, Caelan, what's it like at your house? Got much room?"

I froze. *No, no, no!* Not that I had anything against them ...

"I guess we won't be doing our science presentation any time soon," Klingzong said sadly.

Surely they couldn't be serious? My groan was long and loud. I was really going to cop it for this one. Suddenly, I wished I wasn't going back home, because my parents were going to hit the roof!

How long would these aliens live with me and my family? Probably forever. Or at least until I found a way to get them back.

But when on Earth would that be?